Ellen van Neerven is a Yugambeh woman from South East Queensland. She is the author of *Comfort Food* (UQP, 2016) and *Heat and Light* (UQP, 2014), which won the 2013 David Unaipon Award, the 2015 Dobbie Award and the 2016 NSW Premier's Literary Awards Indigenous Writer's Prize.

Also by Ellen van Neerven

Heat and Light

ELLEN

VAN

NEERVEN

COMFORT

FOOD

UQP

First published 2016 by University of Queensland Press
PO Box 6042, St Lucia, Queensland 4067 Australia
Reprinted 2016, 2017 (twice), 2018

www.uqp.com.au
uqp@uqp.uq.edu.au

Cover design/bunya nut illustration by Josh Durham (Design by Committee)
Author photograph by Bridget Wood
Typeset in 11.5/14 pt Adobe Garamond by Post Pre-press Group, Brisbane
Printed in Australia by McPherson's Printing Group

Quote from the book *MxT* by Sina Queyras © 2014. Reprinted with permission
of Coach House Books, Canada.

Australian Government

Australia Council for the Arts

This project has been assisted by the Australian Government through the Australia
Council for the Arts, its arts funding and advisory body.

Cataloguing-in-Publication entry is available from the National Library of Australia
http://catalogue.nla.gov.au

ISBN 978 0 7022 5405 5 (pbk)
ISBN 978 0 7022 5723 0 (pdf)
ISBN 978 0 7022 5724 7 (epub)
ISBN 978 0 7022 5725 4 (kindle)

For those who have made me meals

Contents

•◦◆◦•

•◦◆◦•

•◦◆◦•

••◗◖••

••◗◖••

I am not interested in other words for honey.
I am interested in honey.

Sina Queyras, *MxT*

Whole Lot

family, earth
dingo, eagle
fire, food
Whole Lot
it's all of those things

what we eat comes from our roots
if we stop sharing there will be nothing

we start with black
let it get hold of you
look at the stars
or are you afraid to?

the day shows
country spread open
a map of all that was and will be
don't forget it
I'm tracing it to remember
don't be scared

we are not here until we sit here
we sit in silence and we are open
there are different kinds of time
I hope you'll understand

sing it
I want this to be here
when I leave again
I've been leaving a lot of times
it doesn't mean I want to
there is no easy way to cry
tell them I'll be back soon
when I come back and sit here
I want to still see Mibunn
powering through the sky

let me tell you with my skin
under the earth we will find
Whole Lot
it's all of those things

Love and Tradition

rising sea
takes and
breaks into backyards
to trouble families

we cannot live
with the seas in our bellies
we cannot rest
with the sea at our legs

the tide
is coming
to stroke
our dead

we want to know
who unplugged
our island
of childhood

island
of love and tradition
let them see
what has gone under

Pinions

I want to know what that hawk got in the grass
What it ate alive
Long grass where a Fogarty, a Sandy, a Currie walked
Shining for bones, a boomerang's hand
'You were the last we expected to do this'
I don't know how I feel, except for mountains
And if they bring the artefacts back
Will we be restored?

Finger Limes

Fingers find finger limes
in my country

We travel to the forest
the morning after rain
my fingers have been cold
in the mornings

We cross the coloured creek
along a patient log
we walk towards frog calls
we walk away from winter

I want to stop on the way back
get some finger limes
I've been homesick for them

But when we return
they are gone
my fingers
numb

We go home anyway
and you make dinner
I'm sorry if I'm crying
I haven't had anyone cook me a meal
it's been a while, you know?

We talk about what we would
and what we wouldn't eat
to stay who we are
for love

I know more
than I can fit into thought
memory is the last defence we have
against cold fingers

Generous

Her mother has just died
but she has bunya nuts
a shopping bag full
and she gives them to me

I fill a bowl of nuts
to take with me upstairs
mostly to keep my hands busy
peeling back nerves

I've been finding it hard
to move through
when you're scared
you're not very generous

She held my shoulder
when I spoke too fast
wanting no-one to hear me
in the surf

To know and to watch her
is to want to be brave
she sat next to me
split us fruit

She will wear any T-shirt
black and blackfulla
put it on her
take it to the streets

Those West End bars
with their pool tables
a lemon lime and bitters
and a good bloody cry

Pasta

When my parents come to stay
I sneak out across the road
to the bathroom at McDonald's
so I don't wake them

Hotel products in the shower
complaints about the weather
Mum hems my jeans
while I'm at work

That night we go to that pasta place
'For nobody's birthday'
we read to each other in the car
condensation at our feet

Pie

caramel
she orders
her daughter-in-law's favourite
she's driving the ks between states
hoping her state of mind too will change
but the bustle of the south-east pocket
doesn't make her feel any more alive
and she hopes the boy at the counter
won't recognise her as
regularly lonely

Bread

Don't tell me what my heart needs, you don't know
that nothing turns me on more than fresh bread

Maybe because my first lover worked in a sandwich bar
got home with the footy crowds, didn't wash
eyes heavy, we still made love
still laughed and drank beer

My lover grew anxious with crowds, hands, cheese knives
gave up the job for the couch
I tried to make love and laugh and drink beer
without the thrill of midnight rye

Two years of buying half bread or splitting it with the freezer
sharpening knives, sleeping with the weather
I'm not yet ready, not even for you
to commit to the $2 whole loaf

Roo Tails

The ground felt like it did when it's about to storm. My feet were brown and my big toe blistered. My grandmother was talking to my grandfather. A wet patch on my grandmother's back. Her hands roping those tails along the fence.

She turned to me and I saw her.

A magpie flew lower.

Prawn Tails

to take the tail of the prawn
squeeze the end
see the licks of liquid
and pull it hard
like the ring
stuck to your finger
at that party
all things come easier
when fresh

Tea

what we left the tea go cold for:
for pleasure
the show you mine if you show me yours
for anger
the fifteen-year-old glare across the table
for running to the subway
the cup still clanging
to the sound of her steps
for grief
a public sobbing
that comes out of everywhere
a family secret
at the touch of lips
let me keep your tea
lukewarm

Mango

eight years old
walking under the bridge
scrub, swamp
abandoned machinery
insides of tennis balls
bits of fences
meeting the boys
at the dam
bikes in a pile
skater shoe soles
not cold in
never is
boys talking about mangoes
slapping water
some have never had one
listen to the taste
the squeeze of a cheek
dripping chins
a dog jumps in
they pull on tufts of hair
fill ears with mud
breeze full
clouds break
they remember my birthday
is tomorrow

Pumpkin

How you make those pumpkin scones so soft? Must've been cos they were Lady Flo's recipe, eh? Pump just melts in your mouth, cut open and have with cheese. Joh's land is never his land, the water sick, the fish die with their original names. Let's rip that tea towel up but keep the recipe, these pump scones the best I ever had. Turn the music down, I left Unc's pumpkin in the car. I left it and I'm away from country.

Chips

can I say
white people really bore me sometimes
to be exact
I grow tired with what's unmentioned
idling in surf club bathrooms
nothing wrong with the chips
but they're talking about Tasmania
my thoughts haunted by islands
I'm maybe dying
I've too many chips
teeth like stones
take me to be flossed
and cleaned
I need new soles
sticking to the floor
what is happening
with the dialogue of this country
they are killing people with words
if I'm not back soon
tell them I've had too many chips

Stamppot

I said I wanted to grow old with you
you said you're already old
you will be in everything I do
even when you go
you've given me too many things
I need things of my own
I'll find ways to keep you, Mum
we'll be on a hard drive in the future
eating stamppot at the house in the bunya forest
with my father

Coffee In Toronto

there was a sense they had slept in shredded aspen
and were now in the city
they didn't look down at the phone as it rang
they didn't
take sugar
he could make fire out of his hands
she sucked ice
the forest was pushing
the wolves and coyotes
coming back

Bagel

her hands covered in cream cheese
and the first snow drops
waiting for the barge to move
a friend's friend's coat
and a friend's friend's scarf
bite off the wind
protect her chest
the island is
the lake's scar
coming closer

Tamale

Finally, a tamale in Texas. She throats her anticipation with a hairclip and another Mexican beer. Corn husk, like Christmas, out of wrapping, out of Toni Price at the Continental. Singled out of the crowd with a slow one but who remembers, graffiti on the toilet door, *every song sounds the same.* Fussed by nothing but the company. The way an evening tumble-turns out of trouble, warm voices, tunnel of black beans, every tamale tastes the same.

Berries

she is of the bear people
so she's first to the berries
it is when original people are acknowledged
the room breathes easier for me
a preoccupation with absence
finding the bears in buildings, universities, public gardens
those who belong to wilderness
take off your socks, show your fur
and I'll show you my feathers

Ceremonial Rice

I meet you outside the school
Not good, you say, and when
I press, you say your family lost a brother today
The wind curls on you as you speak
a young one
You're easy as always with the children
smiling at the bowl of rice in your hands
but I feel the weight when you move
You dance the rhino
stamping out the fire
and when I walk home
I hear more than the wind

Cashew Tree

she is one of those women I can't speak to
shadow women
a combination of envy and lust
when I see her on the bus
in a sparkly sari
my head playing some
old folk song
the silver in her hair
the song continues
through the cashew nut plantations
through the streets of Panaji
the windows open
her hair waving
to the tune
waving to the men
working roads they
won't see finished
everything here seems unfinished
still I watch
with great anticipation
for her to find my eyes

Smoking Chutney

Dance, you're making love. It's the only way you can dance. And you're on the dance floor just to get a closer look. Those hips, yes. That flank. Her hair fragrant and viral. The band also her. The beat mortar and pestle. She's pushing down, grinding those spices in the air. And you keep moving forward. Chest forward. You keep moving back. Don't fall in love if you can't live that love. Don't put that pickled hand on someone else. The closest you get is a shared flight, stopping in Bangalore. She'll smile from the tarmac. Find somewhere to preserve this. An ageless woman, an ageless goodbye.

Goan Fish Curry

I also saw those spirit dogs
and poetry travelled with me
like rivers
I didn't ever eat alone

Comfort Food

I have fourteen hours in Hong Kong. I get 'Hong Kong money'. I buy 'private resting area'. As the door closes, I feel others' privacies bump up against mine. Rooms, it seems, for vomiting, or for fucking. I just need to stretch out. Hot water on my back. Enough to make me weep. I feel funny taking my clothes off. I turn on the darkness.

In the dining area there is real food to eat. Bread and butter pudding. Tomato soup. Nachos. The last time I ate nachos was on K'gari as I watched the sun lie down on the water.

Reel back home.

No sunset in Hong Kong. Grey skyline.

Temptation

those who sit on the window seat
want to be seen
want to be on the stern
of a sampan
want to be everything
the sun is
sharp and star-shaped
be a car that goes past too often
take the sourdough with two hands
be under me
I shouldn't be here again
but I am
my bicycle's against the stairs
and your back is framed for this

Extra Salt

like a bike I'm easy to get up
wheels bounce
frame light but robust
sturdy, practical, mostly reliable
but no-one's looking these days
for second-hand, used
rusty if you're being impolite
I'm not hiding tricks
I don't want to inflict what
I've suffered this time
let's go to the bay
to that fish place I like
touch and talk about our parents
if the heat's still in our heads
there's room for a Billabong
looking out into the peninsula
it won't be late when I take you home
trust me, I'm concentrating
I wouldn't like to let you go by

Real Estate for Writers

The little unit across the road
from the taco joint?
Or the 'high ceiling creativity'
of the woolstore apartment?
I have specific needs
and yes, I'll give you a signed copy
for the building

Bricks and Lightning

It seems I'm always walking
into the scene of a crime
moustached copper
and fuck-off tape
don't look too closely
you won't be able to sleep
I'm new to this building
I live now by the river where
the ducks look like shoes
in the water
I go to the department store
we used to frequent
I look at grocery receipts
to see how I'm saving
and sometimes I get so lonely
I can barely stand it
tonight I wanted you
like the rain wanted the streets
my building was one of two
struck by lightning
a chunk off the top
spilt bricks on the road
I am marked
drop a Google pin into my heart
like they say in Alice
when the Todd floods
must mean I'm staying

Cousins

Taking a break from my usual weekend warfare
I drive with my mother through the shifting rain
into Mununjali country
a roo bounds across the road
we meet at the pub and I order an
egg sandwich, orange muffin and a newspaper
on the last ten years of your life
We are cousins
though we grew up on different sides of the axis
different sides of the moon
got to remember
same grandmother
same grandmother
We don't share memories
You recall a football game against boys
you fell down and
I turned on the fella who did it
This violence sounds
not like me at all
I remember you came to live with us
when your house burnt down
you were amazed at how many socks I had
and you asked me if you went to my school would
you be the only dark girl in your class
This was the first time I realised that
others could see us differently
We drive up to Nana's resting place
in front of Mt Barney
You take the wheel where I am a passenger

My uncle says you'll teach me in a paddock
He seems to know all them old stories
while my mother is quiet
Got to remember
same mother
same mother
Used to the flies now I sit under a gum
This land heals all my city blues
I haven't the language for that
You read me after all this time
I haven't the language for that

Brother

my brother's a moon
he lives at night
his mind is in the shade
of an endless technicolour
he wakes up a drone to the darkness
leaving his didge on the floor
I watched our uncle teach him
in the sweat of an afternoon
now the only rhythm that calls him
is the buzz of the electrical
the technical
blueing
screen eclipses language and
the lunge of thought

Climbers

the hold patterns in the bunya pine
do not fit a hand, or a foot
do not fit hands
or feet anymore
but it is not a wrecked kind of meaning
as trees outgrow us
rivers run dry, tides envelop
weather was always in the news
marks are not wounds

Bruns

you see that black-shouldered kite
diving for secrets in the rocks
our uncle – sick of losing this way
climbs down when he gets his next one
wringing his toes
sinking his knees
hanging on a taunt line
the snapper
shining in the water
the people on the beach
standing up for our uncle
as he walks it
midwifes it in with the tide

Subtitles

mother on the other side of the river
your lips are pressed together
you don't answer my call
a great current
swallowed the sound
future does not hold in subtitles
got to weave that knowledge now
into baskets of stars
a pattern
in song in scarf in eyes
war cries
crocodile and music
and rocks tiptoeing across the river
like unsure words
maybe the hope is just about closing
shadow, green grey outside
when feeling disconnected
see all my family in a boat
at the mouth of the river

Sweet Note

the heart is open and oozing rhubarb
and this lover knows sex is custard
likes it without a recipe

September

You're wearing the pants
that come out in the warmer months
or from the bottom of your ironing pile

I have an uncle who irons all his blackfulla shirts
and a brother his original Roar kit, shorts and all
you're as peculiar as men, I can say that
those pants the colour of last summer's grass
last summer's kisses at the water's edge
you almost got us in

If this is once a year, or once a few
I'll wait
like a mango tree

Flight Feathers

mob of pelicans
big way here
crowding that jetty
like a family photo

don't feel it?
it's bad air

from the top of the lake
to the mountains
is tree war country

light catches pink
throats of conflict

make a boat traditional way and cover this lake
make a desk traditional way and cover this page
we want something back from this water
taste the salt but not
the tears
the pelicans are leaving us
like a line of words
quicker than the tongue
drift   glide   sail   waft
fly
fly away
something happened here

At Musgrave

When the bunya used to be at Musgrave
protection for us mob
take your tea and bikkies
you have been worn
and you have been warned

Let me on stage at Musgrave
hoop pine not the same
read passages that fall the same
I can't emote
so take your vote

Wouldn't recognise him at Musgrave
Aboriginal to some, white to others
I wouldn't know him anymore
the sky may break
the crown still shakes

Meteorite

Your name changes when you land
on earth. What you were is now
your past. The planet
is built for sea-living
but we do not pay
these creatures due respect
the porpoises
          are merely pig fish
the reef
          is a public art gallery
sometimes you stare
at the sky
and wish to be
what you were:

a meteor

Lullaby for a Shark

shark in a tank
you want to sleep
but keep finding
the end too soon
your belly on the
fake sand floor
your bed used to be
three kilometres deep
now you look
beyond the glass
into our eyes
shark ancestor
who created us
we respected you
we shouldn't spoonfeed you water
like gruel to babies
Waryam return
lift Coomera again

Fault

the sleeping giant
they prod and pick
will come after the weak-willed
and power-hungry
the non-thinkers
blank looks and the arguing
arguing that theft is gone
when theft is still the smell
of our rainforests, waters, buildings

out here there's reading to be done
risks to your hygiene
quarantined health and Google mind
a chance to be a piece in time
not a timeline
or a picket in a fence
let's get rid of this border thinking
know that everything has a place
without definition
when things die here
they're meant to die
it's not just a fault
of the human design

ETA

Look, I'd be okay with a shit and a lie-down when I get to yours, thanks. Let's not talk or do anything that could go wrong. It's overcast and I can feel it mist into the train. The trees are so straight. I feel better throwing the city over my shoulder. This week's just an ache, just an ache. It will soon be last week.

Five-Minute Meals

Pan-fried haloumi, bed of greens
Store-bought rice and chilli beans
Five minutes to make it fiery
Miso soup just past expiry
Smashed av, I can't wait
Don't even get out a plate
The quickest noodles on the town
Come on, love, please sit down

How My Heart Behaves

My coin purse is lined
with receipts of women I've fucked and left
Last night on the bed of a lover
slipping a singlet over my breasts
about to leave
I find myself suddenly desiccated
with need of child
Will I always be
a stranger to the sound of softer feet
a moon in the orbit of others
I creep away from her sleeping form
Leave all my change under the pillow

Please Pause Today

I remember my grandfather today.
> *The cultivation of an imperialist invasion of a*
> *foreign nation.*

I remember he fought for this country, for our freedom.
> *Poorly-read, largely white, nationalist drinkers pause,*
> *please pause today.*

Without citizenship, equal rights, equal pay.
> *Summary execution, widespread rape and theft*
> *committed by the brave.*

Denied entry into RSLs, restaurants, taxis,
another entry to the cinema.
> *The largest single-day terrorist attacks committed*
> *by this nation.*

He died without medals.
> *Innocent children killed.*

G20 Free Range

I walk in my singlet
to the city
to brown up
and show up
wearing my flag
on my chest
is warrant
to arrest
my Greek friend
stripped of rights
can't make baklava
without egg whites
and a sense of past
with the packs
like 1890
keep out the blacks
we keep going
to the park
with a fire
for the dark

We're Still Here

Shake a leg
Tie it up
Which way
Breed it out
Kup muri
Shut it up
Point the bone
Keep it out
We're still here

Invisible Spears

a stadium can hold the most sound
drowning out the bora ring
muddying the lines we needed to know
where we're going
now it's a clusterfuck to get the train home
flip-up seats and overflowing beer
the rude odour of tomato sauce
and the black faces they never show on TV
the team with the most blackfullas
they don't want to win
the commentator's curse
the tiddling fear
of invisible spears
we can't score goals
on this sacred land
celebrated as animals
GI doing the goanna, yeah
but not people
with military intelligence
you don't want us protecting
our land like the Maori
that means it was our land to protect
we don't need
a haka of whitefullas
just let us resist

Surfboards

you can name six beaches
where deeper riots started
and haven't finished
man's moral necessity
synthetic polymer surfboards
with a human debt
when does a man
cease to be a man
standing up in the water
rising
standing, making contact
contact
meaning death

Spectra of Birds

in order of the most open
to the most closed
these are our birds
with beaks like milk carton spouts
shake before opening
they come with an expiry date
of three to four years
the tawny frogmouth
is so easy-to-flatten
bassian thrush – chocolate milk
brown cuckoo dove – bronze custard
sooty oystercatcher – tastes better with oil
water your gardens with milk
to neutralise the earth

Future Senses

the dead create now
their thoughts produce like a self-saucing sea

data collects where
oceans collide at the top of Australia

no weather now
not even a summer storm in August

before I couldn't believe people could really go
as you said they do

like the headlights of a car
a drop in temperature as soon as the sun sets

calling a name with
the skin of the sky in my teeth

bats low
in sympathy

we are Facebook friends forever
immortal, and enshrined

we are heat maps
our footprints never fade

we talk and keep talking
smelling water kilometres away

Iris Brides

They said he was mad
and he probably was, when he planted
sixty-one flowering plants on the property
most of them in lines either side of the driveway

It felt like he was coming home to something
and maybe he was less likely to go
show his face at the pub
where they all knew the stories

He chopped his own wood
grew his own food
they stopped bothering him
or he stopped bothering them

A few months passed, no visitors
the plants hadn't flowered
a cold winter without mended socks
he realised they were for Addie

He thought she'd come back
and fill all the little holes
that had come into the cottage
with her needlework, pastry and humming

He had promised her something elegant
instead of children
but hadn't delivered
September had set in

He thought they wouldn't come
wanted to rip them out
to use as kindling
by October he'd forgotten about them

He didn't stare out the window
or see the sun on the door
he didn't go outside at all
even to the great dragon she'd made

The animals came to him
transparent-bellied geckos
hoodlum mice, thirsty frogs
a tree snake hung with his belts

He stopped the fires before summer
even on rainy afternoons
he heard the crash come from the forest
and ran out into the wet

A tree had come down
on Addie's dragon
he didn't know what to do
picked wood and licked his splinters out

On his way back to the house
a patch of iris by the door
purple, white and yellow
like floating lilies in a pond

Like the decorations on cupcakes
that night he cried as he polished
sixty-one wine glasses, opened a bottle
and wished for a wife

He'd sworn they were humming
he moved to the moonlight
started to count them
came to thirty-two

The next day there were forty
and the next week – fifty
by the time he regretted winter
there were sixty-one

In the night they glowed strongly
and he could not leave them
he walked out
and they were women

They drank from the wine glasses
crowded the deck, sang songs
like dreams, they opened only at night
and his heart was a night crime
he tasted their tongues
sixty-one purple iris brides

Summer days were hot arrows
he stole water
put up sails
still they were wilting and going

The phone rang out
news from Thailand
Addie's voice
Could he ... send the dragon back

The snake watched from the roof
he got the kitchen scissors
cut off each of the flowers
hung them on the washing line

In the night their faces were as ugly
as diseased Tasmanian devils
and they screamed like the devils
when their purple and yellow dresses
lost their colour and fell
to be part of the forest

Stomach

she has something in her stomach
says it's gallstones but the ultrasound is clear
did she want children
that day she found a snakeskin by the river
they say grief infiltrates strange locations
usually ties itself around your lungs like rubber bands
she had a lover who took her cancer
put it in a bell jar facing the window
there was the Kate Bush song she ate
the birthdays she missed
the words skipped over
the plants that died
sentimentality about buildings
like the houses they build on the train line
some things can't be saved
where is it
tell me again
a pain low is your gut
a pain higher is your heart

Soft Shell

a king parrot on my birthday
a pale morning
I couldn't have hoped for this
will we talk about
the crab spring rolls
the salmon soup
at the best restaurant in town
how about unbought gifts
the mother and son birds
the counted kisses
the twist of hips

Dalgay/Yugambeh Death Poem

I've been in and out
of the pelican's mouth
I hope they know
what their cruelty meant
I don't want to be
part of the chain
I'm learning self-massage
but I often walk with my hands
behind my back when it's cold
I hadn't the protection of my parents
and I'm disappointed with our land effort
and the misplaced loyalty of kin
I want more as I get older
but I'll never get the years back

                        with my grandmother
I don't speak my language
but I speak yours

                        and I write it well
I haven't yet found the place I will die
and I haven't yet written that poem
the dead tree is already gone
but it will linger in this life

                        for a lifetime
like love

Coconut Oil

I rub coconut oil
onto my knee, already scarred
a one-year scar
unforgiving blemish
strangled by beauty myths
I give birth out of clitoris
shed hair on the beach
go grey at thirty
don't fit into my jeans

Biscuit acne
coffee stains
old bush women guide me
to waterhole
sing my beauty, my strength
rub tea-tree into skin
no mirrors
just water

Freshwater woman, I am
Talgunn, Hairywoman, European, I am
wading in
to the light
make room for my body
naked like muni
three embryos in my womb
waiting for the opportune moment
to begin

Buffalo Milk

suck until you burn the room
and the heat numbs
reduced to a sound
a wet sound
like the come and go of the ocean
water enters
my hand in your hair
my hand
if you leave me childless
this will be yours alone
these marks you make
openings, persuasions
of the woman I will become

Notes

'Whole Lot' was written as a response to Aunty Emily Kame Kngwarreye's iconic painting *Big Yam Dreaming* (1995). Aunty Emily, when asked to explain her paintings, answered, 'Whole lot, that's whole lot, Awelye (my Dreaming), Arlatyeye (pencil yam), Arkerrthe (mountain devil lizard), Ntange (grass seed), Tingu (Dreamtime pup), Ankerre (emu), Intekwe (favourite food of emus, a small plant), Atnwerle (green bean), and Kame (yam seed). That's what I paint, whole lot.'

'How My Heart Behaves' takes its title from the Feist song of the same name.

'Please Pause Today' borrows from ex-SBS journalist Scott McIntyre's 2015 Anzac Day tweets.

'Invisible Spears' is dedicated to Adam Goodes. 'GI' refers to NRL player Greg Inglis, and his goanna crawl try celebration.

'Surfboards' was written as a response to Vernon Ah Kee's artwork *acontentedslave* (2015).

'Spectra of Birds' was written as a response to Madeleine Kelly's artwork *Spectra of Birds* (2014–15).

Acknowledgements

The author would like to thank the editors of the following journals and anthologies for first publishing poems from this collection:

Australian Book Review: 'Temptation'

Cordite Poetry Review: 'Flight Feathers', 'Pinions'

For Rhino in a Shrinking World (UK): 'Ceremonial Rice', 'Meteorite'

From the Outer (Black Inc.): 'Invisible Spears'

Mascara Literary Review: 'Cousins', 'How My Heart Behaves'

National Gallery of Victoria blog: 'Finger Limes', 'Generous', 'Whole Lot'

Overland: 'Invisible Spears'

Queensland Poetry Festival's *<O>PEN*: 'Future Senses'

Australian Book Review's *States of Poetry*: 'Bricks and Lightning', 'Buffalo Milk', 'Chips', 'Love and Tradition', 'Roo Tails'

unmagazine: 'Spectra of Birds', 'Subtitles', 'Surfboards'